EMMANUEL JOSEPH

From Moscow to The Hague, Russia's Complex Relationship with International Law

Copyright © 2025 by Emmanuel Joseph

All rights reserved. No part of this publication may be reproduced, stored or transmitted in any form or by any means, electronic, mechanical, photocopying, recording, scanning, or otherwise without written permission from the publisher. It is illegal to copy this book, post it to a website, or distribute it by any other means without permission.

First edition

This book was professionally typeset on Reedsy. Find out more at reedsy.com

Contents

1. Chapter 1: Introduction to International Law and Russia's...   1
2. Chapter 2: Russia and the United Nations   3
3. Chapter 3: Russia and International Human Rights Law   5
4. Chapter 4: Russia and International Criminal Law   7
5. Chapter 5: Russia and the Law of the Sea   10
6. Chapter 6: Russia and International Environmental Law   12
7. Chapter 7: Russia and International Trade Law   15
8. Chapter 8: Russia and International Security Law   18
9. Chapter 9: Russia and International Humanitarian Law   20
10. Chapter 10: Russia and International Economic Law   22
11. Chapter 11: Russia and International Humanitarian Assistance   25
12. Chapter 12 Russia's Complex Relationship with International...   28

1

Chapter 1: Introduction to International Law and Russia's Historical Context

International law has evolved over centuries, becoming an essential framework for regulating interactions between sovereign states. In the global arena, nations navigate a complex web of treaties, conventions, and legal norms designed to maintain peace and foster cooperation. Understanding Russia's relationship with international law requires delving into its historical context and examining how its geopolitical ambitions have influenced its stance on legal matters. From the era of the Russian Empire to the Soviet Union and modern-day Russia, each period has seen distinct shifts in attitudes and strategies toward international law.

Historically, Russia's expansive territory and strategic interests have driven its engagement with international law. The nation's vast geography, bordering multiple countries and spanning two continents, has necessitated diplomatic and legal interactions on various fronts. During the Russian Empire, the monarchy wielded considerable influence in shaping international agreements, often prioritizing territorial expansion and consolidation of power. This imperial approach laid the groundwork for Russia's later interactions with international law.

The Soviet era marked a significant departure from traditional legal norms, as the USSR sought to redefine international law to align with its ideological goals. The Cold War era saw the Soviets advocating for a socialist interpretation of international law, often challenging Western legal principles and promoting a distinct legal order. This period was characterized by a complex interplay of cooperation and confrontation, with the Soviet Union actively participating in international organizations while simultaneously asserting its sovereignty and ideological stance.

Post-Soviet Russia inherited a legacy of legal complexities and geopolitical ambitions. The collapse of the USSR in 1991 led to a period of transition and reorientation in Russia's foreign policy. The newly independent Russian Federation faced the task of integrating into the existing international legal framework while asserting its interests on the global stage. This transition period witnessed Russia's engagement with various international treaties and conventions, as it sought to establish itself as a key player in the post-Cold War world order.

In the contemporary era, Russia's relationship with international law continues to be shaped by its strategic interests and geopolitical considerations. The annexation of Crimea in 2014 and subsequent conflicts in Ukraine have brought Russia's adherence to international legal norms into sharp focus. These events have sparked debates about the interpretation and enforcement of international law, highlighting the complexities and challenges of maintaining a rules-based international order in the face of evolving geopolitical dynamics.

2

Chapter 2: Russia and the United Nations

Russia's role in the United Nations (UN) has been instrumental in shaping its relationship with international law. As a founding member of the UN and a permanent member of the Security Council, Russia wields significant influence in the organization. This chapter explores Russia's participation in the UN, its contributions to international peace and security, and the challenges it faces in balancing its national interests with its responsibilities as a global actor.

From the outset, Russia's membership in the UN was driven by its desire to secure a prominent position in the post-World War II international order. The Soviet Union played a crucial role in the establishment of the UN, advocating for a system that would prevent future conflicts and promote cooperation among nations. The inclusion of the USSR as a permanent member of the Security Council, with veto power, underscored its importance in maintaining global peace and security.

Throughout the Cold War, the Soviet Union's interactions with the UN were marked by a dual approach of cooperation and competition. While actively participating in UN initiatives and contributing to peacekeeping efforts, the USSR often found itself at odds with Western powers, particularly the United States. The Security Council became a battleground for ideological clashes, with the Soviet Union using its veto power to block resolutions that conflicted with its interests and advocating for an alternative vision of international law.

The dissolution of the Soviet Union in 1991 brought about significant changes in Russia's approach to the UN. As the successor state, the Russian Federation inherited the USSR's seat on the Security Council and continued to play a pivotal role in the organization. The post-Soviet period saw Russia adopting a more pragmatic approach to international law, seeking to balance its national interests with its obligations as a UN member. This period also witnessed Russia's increased participation in peacekeeping missions and its support for multilateralism.

In recent years, Russia's relationship with the UN has been shaped by evolving geopolitical dynamics and its assertive foreign policy. The Syrian conflict and the annexation of Crimea have highlighted Russia's willingness to use its veto power to protect its interests and challenge Western-led initiatives. These actions have sparked debates about the effectiveness of the Security Council and the broader implications for international law. Despite these challenges, Russia continues to engage with the UN, emphasizing the importance of dialogue and cooperation in addressing global issues.

Russia's participation in the UN exemplifies the complexities of its relationship with international law. As a major global actor, Russia's actions within the UN framework reflect its strategic interests and its vision for the international order. While often at odds with Western powers, Russia's engagement with the UN underscores its commitment to multilateralism and its recognition of the organization's role in maintaining global peace and security.

3

Chapter 3: Russia and International Human Rights Law

International human rights law is a crucial aspect of the global legal framework, aimed at protecting the fundamental rights and freedoms of individuals. This chapter delves into Russia's relationship with international human rights law, examining its commitments, compliance, and challenges in upholding these principles. The analysis focuses on Russia's participation in human rights treaties, its interactions with international human rights bodies, and the domestic implications of international human rights norms.

Russia's engagement with international human rights law dates back to the Soviet era, when the USSR became a party to several key human rights treaties, including the International Covenant on Civil and Political Rights (ICCPR) and the International Covenant on Economic, Social, and Cultural Rights (ICESCR). These commitments were part of the broader effort to enhance the USSR's international standing and demonstrate its adherence to global norms. However, the Soviet regime's authoritarian nature and its focus on state control often resulted in a selective and inconsistent application of human rights principles.

The post-Soviet period marked a significant shift in Russia's approach to international human rights law. The newly independent Russian Federation sought to integrate itself into the global community by ratifying various human rights treaties and participating in international human rights mechanisms. Russia's accession to the European Convention on Human Rights (ECHR) and its recognition of the jurisdiction of the European Court of Human Rights (ECtHR) were notable milestones in this process. These steps reflected Russia's commitment to aligning its legal system with international human rights standards.

Despite these formal commitments, Russia's compliance with international human rights law has faced numerous challenges. The domestic legal and political landscape has often hindered the effective implementation of human rights norms. Issues such as restrictions on freedom of expression, assembly, and the press, as well as concerns about the independence of the judiciary, have raised questions about Russia's adherence to its international obligations. Human rights organizations and activists have frequently criticized the Russian government for its actions, calling for greater accountability and reforms.

Russia's interactions with international human rights bodies have been complex and, at times, contentious. The European Court of Human Rights has issued numerous judgments against Russia, addressing violations of the ECHR. While Russia has complied with some of these rulings, there have been instances of resistance and non-compliance, particularly in cases involving politically sensitive issues. Additionally, Russia's response to international human rights criticisms has often been defensive, framing such critiques as attempts to undermine its sovereignty and internal affairs.

In conclusion, Russia's relationship with international human rights law is marked by a combination of formal commitments and practical challenges. While the country has made significant strides in integrating international human rights norms into its legal framework, persistent issues and domestic constraints continue to impact its compliance. The complex interplay between international legal obligations and domestic realities underscores the ongoing challenges in upholding human rights in Russia.

4

Chapter 4: Russia and International Criminal Law

International criminal law aims to hold individuals accountable for the most serious crimes, such as genocide, war crimes, and crimes against humanity. This chapter explores Russia's relationship with international criminal law, focusing on its stance toward the International Criminal Court (ICC), its involvement in international criminal tribunals, and its domestic efforts to address international crimes. The analysis also considers the political and legal factors that influence Russia's approach to international criminal justice.

Russia's engagement with international criminal law has been shaped by historical and geopolitical considerations. During the Nuremberg Trials after World War II, the Soviet Union played a key role in prosecuting Nazi war criminals, contributing to the development of international criminal law. The Soviet experience at Nuremberg influenced its subsequent approach to international criminal justice, emphasizing state sovereignty and the protection of national interests.

The establishment of the International Criminal Court in 2002 marked a significant development in the field of international criminal law. However, Russia's relationship with the ICC has been complex and, at times, contentious. While Russia signed the Rome Statute, the treaty that established the ICC, in 2000, it has not ratified it, citing concerns about the court's jurisdiction and potential political bias. Russia's withdrawal of its signature from the Rome Statute in 2016 further underscored its reservations about the ICC and its commitment to maintaining sovereignty over criminal justice matters.

Despite its reservations about the ICC, Russia has participated in other international criminal justice mechanisms. For instance, Russia supported the establishment of the International Criminal Tribunal for the former Yugoslavia (ICTY) and the International Criminal Tribunal for Rwanda (ICTR), contributing to the prosecution of individuals responsible for serious international crimes. Additionally, Russia has advocated for accountability in cases involving terrorism and other transnational crimes, highlighting the need for international cooperation in addressing such threats.

Domestically, Russia has made efforts to address international crimes through its legal system. The Russian Criminal Code includes provisions for prosecuting war crimes, genocide, and other serious offenses. However, the effectiveness of these efforts has been questioned, particularly in cases involving allegations of crimes committed by Russian nationals or state actors. Concerns about the independence of the judiciary and the politicization of criminal justice have further complicated Russia's complex and multifaceted relationship with international criminal law. The Russian Criminal Code includes provisions for prosecuting war crimes, genocide, and other serious offenses. However, the effectiveness of these efforts has been questioned, particularly in cases involving allegations of crimes committed by Russian nationals or state actors. Concerns about the independence of the judiciary and the politicization of criminal justice have further complicated Russia's domestic efforts to address international crimes.

In high-profile cases involving international crimes, Russia has faced criticism from both domestic and international actors. For example, the investigation and prosecution of individuals involved in the downing of Malaysia Airlines Flight MH17 over eastern Ukraine have been contentious. Russia's refusal to cooperate with international investigations and its rejection of the findings of the Joint Investigation Team (JIT) have highlighted the challenges of achieving accountability in such cases. These incidents underscore the tension between Russia's assertions of sovereignty and the principles of international criminal justice.

Despite these challenges, Russia has continued to engage with international criminal law on its own terms. The country's stance towards the ICC and other international criminal justice mechanisms reflects its broader approach to international law: a careful balancing act between maintaining national sovereignty and engaging with the global legal order. As the international community continues to grapple with the complexities of prosecuting international crimes, Russia's role in this evolving landscape remains a critical factor in shaping the future of international criminal justice.

5

Chapter 5: Russia and the Law of the Sea

The Law of the Sea is a critical component of international law, governing maritime activities and delineating the rights and responsibilities of states in their use of the world's oceans. This chapter examines Russia's relationship with the Law of the Sea, focusing on its involvement in maritime disputes, its role in the United Nations Convention on the Law of the Sea (UNCLOS), and its strategic interests in the Arctic region.

Russia's maritime interests are deeply intertwined with its geopolitical and economic aspirations. As one of the largest coastal states, with access to the Arctic Ocean, the Baltic Sea, the Black Sea, and the Pacific Ocean, Russia has a vested interest in the regulation of maritime activities. The Soviet Union was actively involved in the negotiations leading to the adoption of UNCLOS in 1982, and Russia, as its successor state, ratified the convention in 1997. UNCLOS provides a comprehensive legal framework for maritime governance, including provisions on territorial seas, exclusive economic zones (EEZs), and continental shelves.

One of the key areas of focus in Russia's maritime strategy is the Arctic region. The melting of Arctic ice due to climate change has opened up new possibilities for resource exploration and navigation. Russia has been assertive in its claims to the Arctic continental shelf, seeking to extend its jurisdiction over vast areas of the Arctic Ocean. This has led to disputes with other Arctic states, such as Canada, Denmark, and Norway, which have competing claims. Russia's submission to the United Nations Commission on the Limits of the Continental Shelf (CLCS) in 2001 and subsequent efforts to strengthen its Arctic presence reflect its strategic priorities in the region.

In addition to its Arctic ambitions, Russia has been involved in various maritime disputes, particularly in the Black Sea and the Sea of Azov. The annexation of Crimea in 2014 and the subsequent conflict with Ukraine have heightened tensions in these waters. Russia's actions, including the construction of the Kerch Strait Bridge and the detention of Ukrainian vessels, have raised concerns about freedom of navigation and adherence to international maritime law. These disputes have underscored the challenges of balancing national security interests with the principles of the Law of the Sea.

Russia's participation in international maritime organizations and forums highlights its commitment to engaging with the global legal order while pursuing its strategic interests. As a member of the International Maritime Organization (IMO) and other bodies, Russia has contributed to the development of maritime safety standards and environmental regulations. However, its actions in contested maritime areas have occasionally brought it into conflict with other states and international legal norms.

Overall, Russia's relationship with the Law of the Sea is characterized by a complex interplay of cooperation and competition. While actively participating in international maritime governance, Russia continues to assert its sovereignty and strategic interests, particularly in regions of geopolitical significance. As the maritime landscape evolves, Russia's approach to the Law of the Sea will remain a critical factor in shaping the future of international maritime law.

6

Chapter 6: Russia and International Environmental Law

International environmental law has become increasingly important in addressing global challenges such as climate change, biodiversity loss, and pollution. This chapter explores Russia's engagement with international environmental law, focusing on its participation in key environmental treaties, its domestic environmental policies, and the challenges it faces in balancing economic development with environmental protection.

Russia's vast and diverse geography, encompassing forests, rivers, lakes, and arctic tundra, makes it a significant player in global environmental governance. The country's natural resources, including oil, gas, minerals, and timber, are critical to its economy, but their extraction and use have significant environmental implications. Russia's participation in international environmental treaties reflects its recognition of the importance of addressing global environmental issues while protecting its national interests.

One of the key milestones in Russia's engagement with international environmental law was its ratification of the Kyoto Protocol in 2004. The protocol, which aimed to reduce greenhouse gas emissions and mitigate climate change, marked a significant step in Russia's commitment to global environmental efforts. Russia's role in the Kyoto Protocol was crucial in

CHAPTER 6: RUSSIA AND INTERNATIONAL ENVIRONMENTAL LAW

ensuring the treaty's entry into force, as its participation was necessary to meet the threshold for global emissions coverage. Despite this, Russia's approach to climate change has been characterized by a careful balancing act between economic development and environmental protection.

Russia's domestic environmental policies have faced numerous challenges, including pollution, deforestation, and the impact of industrial activities on ecosystems. The country has implemented various measures to address these issues, such as the establishment of protected areas, regulations on industrial emissions, and initiatives to promote renewable energy. However, the effectiveness of these measures has been questioned, particularly in light of the country's reliance on fossil fuels and the influence of powerful industrial interests.

In the international arena, Russia has participated in various environmental agreements and forums, contributing to the development of global environmental governance. As a member of the United Nations Framework Convention on Climate Change (UNFCCC), the Convention on Biological Diversity (CBD), and other treaties, Russia has engaged in negotiations and initiatives aimed at addressing pressing environmental challenges. However, the country's actions have sometimes been criticized for prioritizing economic interests over environmental protection.

The Arctic region, with its unique and fragile ecosystem, has been a focal point of Russia's environmental policies. The melting of Arctic ice due to climate change has created both opportunities and risks for Russia, with potential for resource exploration and new shipping routes, but also significant environmental threats. Russia has sought to balance these competing interests by advocating for sustainable development in the Arctic and participating in regional environmental cooperation through the Arctic Council.

In conclusion, Russia's relationship with international environmental law is marked by a combination of formal commitments and practical challenges. While the country has made significant strides in participating in global environmental governance, domestic and international constraints continue to impact its ability to fully address environmental issues. The complex interplay between economic development and environmental protection underscores the ongoing challenges in ensuring sustainable development in Russia.

7

Chapter 7: Russia and International Trade Law

International trade law governs the rules and regulations that facilitate trade between nations, promoting economic growth and cooperation. This chapter examines Russia's relationship with international trade law, focusing on its participation in the World Trade Organization (WTO), its trade policies, and the challenges it faces in navigating the global trading system.

Russia's integration into the global trading system has been a gradual and complex process, influenced by historical, economic, and political factors. The collapse of the Soviet Union in 1991 marked the beginning of a significant transformation in Russia's trade policies, as the country sought to transition from a centrally planned economy to a market-oriented one. This period of transition was characterized by efforts to liberalize trade, attract foreign investment, and integrate into the global economy.

A key milestone in Russia's engagement with international trade law was its accession to the World Trade Organization in 2012. The WTO provides a comprehensive legal framework for international trade, encompassing rules on tariffs, trade in services, intellectual property, and dispute resolution. Russia's membership in the WTO marked a significant step in its efforts to align its trade policies with global standards and promote economic growth through increased trade and investment.

Russia's participation in the WTO has been accompanied by both opportunities and challenges. On the one hand, WTO membership has provided Russia with greater access to global markets, enabling it to expand its exports of energy, minerals, and agricultural products. On the other hand, Russia has faced challenges in complying with WTO rules, particularly in areas such as state subsidies, intellectual property protection, and trade-related environmental measures. These challenges have sometimes led to disputes with other WTO members, highlighting the complexities of navigating the global trading system.

In addition to its engagement with the WTO, Russia has pursued regional trade initiatives to strengthen its economic ties with neighboring countries. The establishment of the Eurasian Economic Union (EAEU) in 2015, which includes Russia, Belarus, Kazakhstan, Armenia, and Kyrgyzstan, reflects Russia's efforts to promote regional economic integration and create a common market for goods, services, capital, and labor. The EAEU has implemented various trade agreements and policies aimed at facilitating intra-regional trade and attracting investment.

Despite these efforts, Russia's trade policies have sometimes been influenced by geopolitical considerations, leading to tensions with other countries. The imposition of economic sanctions by Western countries following the annexation of Crimea in 2014 and Russia's subsequent counter-sanctions have had a significant impact on its trade relations. These actions have highlighted the intersection of trade and politics, underscoring the challenges of maintaining stable and predictable trade policies in a volatile geopolitical environment.

Overall, Russia's relationship with international trade law is characterized by a dynamic interplay of cooperation and competition. While actively participating in the global trading system, Russia continues to navigate the complexities of complying navigating the complexities of complying with international trade regulations while safeguarding its national interests. This balance is crucial for fostering economic growth and maintaining Russia's strategic position in the global economy.

CHAPTER 7: RUSSIA AND INTERNATIONAL TRADE LAW

Russia's trade policies and strategies have been shaped by its historical experiences and geopolitical environment. The legacy of the Soviet Union's command economy and its subsequent transition to a market-oriented system have influenced Russia's approach to trade. The pursuit of economic diversification, technological advancement, and integration into global value chains remains a key priority for the Russian government. However, achieving these goals requires addressing structural challenges, such as bureaucracy, corruption, and infrastructure deficiencies.

In its efforts to expand trade and investment, Russia has sought to establish and strengthen trade relationships with various regions, including Europe, Asia, and Africa. The country's participation in initiatives such as the Belt and Road Initiative (BRI) and its strategic partnerships with countries like China and India reflect its desire to diversify its trade partners and reduce dependency on any single market. These efforts are aimed at enhancing Russia's economic resilience and promoting sustainable development.

The impact of economic sanctions on Russia's trade relations cannot be overlooked. The imposition of sanctions by Western countries in response to geopolitical tensions, particularly following the annexation of Crimea, has significantly affected Russia's access to international markets and financial systems. In response, Russia has implemented counter-sanctions and pursued import substitution policies to reduce its reliance on foreign goods and technologies. These measures have had mixed results, highlighting the challenges of navigating a complex and interconnected global economy.

Looking ahead, Russia's relationship with international trade law will continue to evolve in response to changing economic and geopolitical dynamics. As the global trading system faces increasing uncertainties, Russia's ability to adapt and innovate will be crucial in shaping its future trade policies. The interplay between national interests and international legal obligations will remain a defining feature of Russia's engagement with the global economy.

8

Chapter 8: Russia and International Security Law

International security law encompasses the legal frameworks and norms that govern the use of force, disarmament, and collective security. This chapter explores Russia's relationship with international security law, focusing on its participation in arms control treaties, its role in regional security arrangements, and its stance on the use of force in international relations.

Russia's engagement with international security law has been shaped by its historical experiences and strategic considerations. The legacy of the Cold War and the subsequent dissolution of the Soviet Union have influenced Russia's approach to arms control and disarmament. The country's participation in key arms control treaties, such as the Treaty on the Non-Proliferation of Nuclear Weapons (NPT), the Intermediate-Range Nuclear Forces (INF) Treaty, and the New Strategic Arms Reduction Treaty (New START), reflects its commitment to maintaining strategic stability and preventing the proliferation of weapons of mass destruction.

Despite these commitments, Russia's compliance with arms control agreements has faced challenges. The suspension of the INF Treaty in 2019 and concerns about the future of New START have raised questions about the stability of the international arms control regime. Russia's development of new weapons systems and its modernization of its nuclear arsenal have further complicated efforts to achieve disarmament and arms control. These actions highlight the tensions between Russia's security interests and its international legal obligations.

In addition to arms control, Russia's role in regional security arrangements has been a key aspect of its engagement with international security law. The Collective Security Treaty Organization (CSTO) and the Shanghai Cooperation Organization (SCO) are two regional security alliances in which Russia plays a leading role. These organizations aim to promote regional stability, combat terrorism and transnational threats, and enhance cooperation among member states. Russia's involvement in these alliances reflects its strategic interests in maintaining influence in its neighboring regions and addressing security challenges through multilateral frameworks.

Russia's stance on the use of force in international relations has been a contentious issue, particularly in light of its actions in Georgia, Ukraine, and Syria. The principles of non-intervention and respect for sovereignty, enshrined in the United Nations Charter, have been central to international security law. However, Russia's military interventions and support for separatist movements have raised questions about its adherence to these principles. These actions have sparked debates about the interpretation and application of international security law, highlighting the complexities of maintaining global peace and security in a multipolar world.

Overall, Russia's relationship with international security law is characterized by a complex interplay of cooperation and competition. While actively participating in arms control and regional security arrangements, Russia continues to assert its strategic interests and navigate the challenges of complying with international legal norms. The evolving geopolitical landscape and the emergence of new security threats will shape Russia's future engagement with international security law.

9

Chapter 9: Russia and International Humanitarian Law

International humanitarian law (IHL), also known as the law of armed conflict, governs the conduct of hostilities and aims to protect individuals who are not participating in the conflict, such as civilians and prisoners of war. This chapter examines Russia's relationship with international humanitarian law, focusing on its adherence to IHL principles, its participation in international humanitarian initiatives, and the challenges it faces in upholding these norms in conflict situations.

Russia's engagement with international humanitarian law dates back to the late 19th and early 20th centuries, when the Russian Empire participated in the Hague Conventions, which established key principles of IHL. The Soviet Union continued this engagement, becoming a party to the Geneva Conventions and their Additional Protocols, which form the core of modern IHL. These treaties outline the rules for the protection of civilians, the wounded and sick, and prisoners of war, as well as the conduct of hostilities.

Despite its formal commitments to IHL, Russia's adherence to these principles has faced challenges in practice. The conduct of Russian forces in various conflicts, including the Chechen wars, the conflict in Georgia, and the ongoing conflict in Ukraine, has raised concerns about compliance with IHL. Allegations of indiscriminate attacks, targeting of civilians, and other violations have been documented by international organizations and human rights groups. These incidents underscore the difficulties of ensuring adherence to IHL in complex and asymmetrical conflicts.

Russia's participation in international humanitarian initiatives reflects its recognition of the importance of addressing humanitarian needs in conflict situations. The country has supported and contributed to various United Nations humanitarian efforts, including peacekeeping missions and disaster relief operations. Additionally, Russia has engaged with the International Committee of the Red Cross (ICRC) and other humanitarian organizations to provide assistance to affected populations. These efforts highlight Russia's commitment to mitigating the humanitarian impact of conflicts and promoting the principles of IHL.

The challenges of upholding IHL in modern conflicts are not unique to Russia. The changing nature of warfare, characterized by the use of advanced technologies, non-state actors, and asymmetrical tactics, has complicated the application of IHL principles. Ensuring compliance with IHL requires a concerted effort by all parties to a conflict, as well as robust mechanisms for accountability and enforcement. Russia's experiences in conflict situations underscore the need for continued engagement with international humanitarian law and the strengthening of IHL frameworks.

In conclusion, Russia's relationship with international humanitarian law is marked by a combination of formal commitments and practical challenges. While the country has made significant strides in participating in global humanitarian initiatives, ensuring adherence to IHL principles in conflict situations remains a complex and ongoing effort. The evolving nature of warfare and the emergence of new humanitarian challenges will shape Russia's future engagement with international humanitarian law.

10

Chapter 10: Russia and International Economic Law

International economic law encompasses the legal frameworks that govern economic relations between states, including trade, investment, and financial regulations. This chapter explores Russia's relationship with international economic law, focusing on its participation in international economic organizations, its investment policies, and the challenges it faces in navigating the global economic landscape.

Russia's integration into the global economy has been a gradual and multifaceted process, influenced by historical, economic, and political factors. The collapse of the Soviet Union and the subsequent transition to a market-oriented economy marked a significant shift in Russia's approach to international economic law. The country sought to attract foreign investment, liberalize trade, and integrate into the global financial system as part of its broader economic transformation.

A key aspect of Russia's engagement with international economic law has been its participation in international economic organizations. In addition to its membership in the World Trade Organization (WTO), Russia is a member of the International Monetary Fund (IMF), the World Bank, and the Group of Twenty (G20). These organizations provide platforms for international economic cooperation, policy coordination, and dispute resolution. Russia's

CHAPTER 10: RUSSIA AND INTERNATIONAL ECONOMIC LAW

participation in these organizations reflects its commitment to engaging with the global economic order and addressing shared economic challenges.

Russia's investment policies have been shaped by the need to balance attracting foreign investment with protecting national interests. The country has implemented various measures to create a favorable investment climate, including regulatory reforms, tax incentives, and infrastructure development. However, challenges such as bureaucracy, corruption, and geopolitical tensions have sometimes hindered the effectiveness of these measures. Ensuring a stable and predictable investment environment remains a key priority for Russia's economic policymakers.

The global economic landscape is characterized by increasing interdependence and complexity, presenting both opportunities and challenges for Russia. The country has sought to diversify its economic partnerships and reduce its reliance on any single market. Initiatives such as the Eurasian Economic Union (EAEU) and strategic partnerships with countries in Asia, Africa, and Latin America reflect Russia's efforts to strengthen its economic resilience and expand its global economic footprint.

Economic sanctions imposed by Western countries in response to geopolitical tensions have had a significant impact on Russia's economic relations. In response, Russia has pursued import substitution policies, promoted domestic industries, and sought alternative markets to mitigate the effects of sanctions. These measures have underscored the challenges of navigating the complexities of international economic law in a volatile geopolitical environment.

Overall, Russia's relationship with international economic law is characterized by a dynamic interplay of cooperation and competition. While actively participating in the global economic order, Russia continues to navigate the challenges of complying with international economic regulations while safeguarding its national interests. The continuation of Russia's relationship with international economic law underscores the need for strategic adaptation and resilience in the face of evolving global dynamics. As the global economy becomes increasingly interconnected, Russia's ability to navigate international economic regulations and maintain its competitive edge will be crucial for its future growth and development.

Russia's participation in international economic organizations and initiatives highlights its commitment to engaging with the global economic order. The country's involvement in forums such as the BRICS (Brazil, Russia, India, China, and South Africa) and the Shanghai Cooperation Organization (SCO) reflects its efforts to foster economic cooperation and strengthen regional economic ties. These initiatives provide platforms for dialogue, collaboration, and the development of common strategies to address shared economic challenges.

In addition to its participation in multilateral organizations, Russia has pursued bilateral trade agreements with various countries to enhance its economic partnerships. These agreements aim to reduce trade barriers, promote investment, and facilitate the exchange of goods and services. Russia's trade agreements with countries in Asia, Europe, and the Middle East are indicative of its efforts to diversify its economic relationships and reduce dependency on any single market.

Despite these efforts, Russia faces several challenges in its engagement with international economic law. The country's reliance on natural resources, such as oil and gas, makes it vulnerable to fluctuations in global commodity prices and external economic shocks. Diversifying the economy and promoting innovation and technological advancement are essential for achieving long-term economic stability and growth. Addressing structural issues, such as corruption, bureaucracy, and infrastructure deficiencies, is also critical for creating a favorable investment climate and enhancing Russia's competitiveness in the global economy.

In conclusion, Russia's relationship with international economic law is characterized by a dynamic interplay of cooperation and competition. While actively participating in the global economic order, Russia continues to navigate the complexities of complying with international economic regulations while safeguarding its national interests. The evolving global economic landscape presents both opportunities and challenges for Russia, requiring strategic adaptation and resilience to maintain its position in the international economic arena.

11

Chapter 11: Russia and International Humanitarian Assistance

International humanitarian assistance encompasses the provision of aid and support to populations affected by crises, such as natural disasters, armed conflicts, and humanitarian emergencies. This chapter explores Russia's engagement with international humanitarian assistance, focusing on its contributions to global humanitarian efforts, its participation in international humanitarian organizations, and the challenges it faces in delivering effective aid.

Russia's commitment to international humanitarian assistance is rooted in its recognition of the importance of addressing humanitarian needs and promoting global solidarity. The country has a long history of providing aid to populations affected by crises, both within its own borders and internationally. Russia's humanitarian assistance efforts are coordinated through various government agencies, non-governmental organizations (NGOs), and international partnerships.

One of the key aspects of Russia's engagement with international humanitarian assistance is its participation in United Nations humanitarian initiatives. As a member of the United Nations Office for the Coordination of Humanitarian Affairs (OCHA) and other UN agencies, Russia has contributed to various humanitarian response efforts, including disaster relief, food security, and health interventions. Russia's financial contributions, logistical support, and deployment of humanitarian personnel reflect its commitment to global humanitarian efforts.

In addition to its participation in UN initiatives, Russia has provided bilateral humanitarian assistance to countries affected by crises. For example, Russia has delivered aid to countries affected by natural disasters, such as earthquakes, floods, and wildfires. The country's response to the Syrian conflict, including the provision of medical supplies, food, and shelter to displaced populations, highlights its efforts to address humanitarian needs in conflict-affected regions. These bilateral aid efforts are often coordinated through the Russian Ministry of Emergency Situations (EMERCOM) and other relevant agencies.

Despite its contributions to international humanitarian assistance, Russia faces several challenges in delivering effective aid. The complexities of coordinating humanitarian responses, ensuring the timely delivery of aid, and addressing the specific needs of affected populations require robust planning and collaboration. Additionally, geopolitical considerations and diplomatic relations can influence the scope and scale of Russia's humanitarian assistance efforts. Ensuring transparency, accountability, and adherence to humanitarian principles are critical for enhancing the effectiveness of aid delivery.

Russia's engagement with international humanitarian organizations and NGOs also plays a significant role in its humanitarian assistance efforts. Partnerships with organizations such as the International Federation of Red Cross and Red Crescent Societies (IFRC) and various humanitarian NGOs facilitate the delivery of aid and support to affected populations. These collaborations enhance Russia's capacity to respond to humanitarian crises and contribute to the broader international humanitarian response system.

In conclusion, Russia's relationship with international humanitarian assistance is characterized by a combination of formal commitments and practical challenges. While the country has made significant strides in participating in global humanitarian efforts, delivering effective aid requires continued collaboration, strategic planning, and adherence to humanitarian principles.

CHAPTER 11: RUSSIA AND INTERNATIONAL HUMANITARIAN ASSISTANCE

The evolving nature of humanitarian crises and the increasing demand for international assistance underscore the importance of Russia's ongoing engagement with international humanitarian organizations and initiatives.

12

Chapter 12 Russia's Complex Relationship with International Law

Russia's relationship with international law is a multifaceted and evolving dynamic shaped by its historical experiences, geopolitical ambitions, and strategic interests. This chapter synthesizes the key themes and insights from the preceding chapters, providing a comprehensive understanding of how Russia navigates the complex landscape of international law.

Throughout its history, Russia has demonstrated a pragmatic and strategic approach to international law. The legacy of the Russian Empire, the ideological stance of the Soviet Union, and the assertive foreign policy of the modern Russian Federation have all influenced the country's interactions with international legal norms. Russia's engagement with international law is characterized by a careful balancing act between maintaining national sovereignty and fulfilling its global responsibilities.

As a major global actor, Russia's actions and decisions within the framework of international law have significant implications for the international community. From its participation in the United Nations and international human rights treaties to its stance on international criminal law and the Law of the Sea, Russia's approach to international legal matters reflects its broader strategic priorities. The country's role in shaping the international legal order

CHAPTER 12 RUSSIA'S COMPLEX RELATIONSHIP WITH INTERNATIONAL...

is underscored by its participation in key international organizations and its contributions to global governance.

However, Russia's adherence to international legal norms has often faced challenges and controversies. Instances of non-compliance with international human rights standards, allegations of violations of international humanitarian law, and disputes over maritime boundaries have raised questions about Russia's commitment to upholding international legal principles. These challenges highlight the tension between Russia's national interests and the expectations of the international community.

Looking ahead, Russia's relationship with international law will continue to evolve in response to changing geopolitical dynamics and emerging global challenges. The country's ability to navigate these complexities and engage constructively with the international legal order will be crucial in shaping its future role on the global stage. As the world faces new and interconnected challenges, from climate change to cyber threats, Russia's engagement with international law will remain a critical factor in promoting global stability and cooperation.

In conclusion, Russia's complex relationship with international law is a reflection of its historical legacy, strategic ambitions, and evolving geopolitical context. By understanding the multifaceted nature of this relationship, we gain valuable insights into the broader dynamics of international law and the challenges of maintaining a rules-based international order in a rapidly changing world.

From Moscow to The Hague: Russia's Complex Relationship with International Law

In "From Moscow to The Hague: Russia's Complex Relationship with International Law," this book provides a comprehensive exploration of Russia's evolving engagement with international law through various historical, geopolitical, and strategic lenses. The narrative unfolds across twelve well-structured chapters, each delving into a distinct facet of Russia's interactions with international legal norms and institutions.

From its early contributions to the development of international humanitarian law to its contemporary participation in key global organizations like

www.ingramcontent.com/pod-product-compliance
Lightning Source LLC
LaVergne TN
LVHW021048100526
838202LV00079B/4777

the United Nations and the World Trade Organization, Russia's journey is both intricate and dynamic. The book sheds light on pivotal moments, such as the Soviet Union's role in shaping the post-World War II order and Russia's integration into the global economic system following the collapse of the USSR.

Key themes include Russia's involvement in international human rights law, its stance on international criminal justice, and the impact of geopolitical events like the annexation of Crimea on its adherence to international legal principles. The book also addresses Russia's strategic interests in the Arctic, its challenges in upholding international humanitarian law in conflict situations, and its complex relationship with international trade regulations amidst economic sanctions.

Through a combination of historical analysis, case studies, and examination of legal frameworks, "From Moscow to The Hague" offers a nuanced understanding of how Russia navigates the intricate web of international law. It highlights the tension between national sovereignty and global responsibilities, providing valuable insights into the broader dynamics of international relations and the challenges of maintaining a rules-based international order in a rapidly changing world.